gauguin's notebook

Christopher Rey Pérez

First published 2017 by &NOW Books, an
imprint of Lake Forest College Press.

Carnegie Hall
Lake Forest College
555 N. Sheridan Road
Lake Forest, IL 60045

lakeforest.edu/andnow

Lake Forest College Press publishes in the broad spaces of
Chicago studies. Our imprint, &NOW Books, publishes
innovative and conceptual literature and serves as the publishing
arm of the &NOW writers' conference and organization.

ISBN: 978-1-941423-96-7

Book and cover design by Rachel Tenuta

Printed in the United States

LAKE FOREST
COLLEGE
PRESS

INTRODUCTION

BY ELENI SIKELIANOS

What if bad angels deface your barcodes, hack your hash tags and mess up your borders? Pull your silver life-bone out of your neck? What if they erase the contours of your representation of life? What if they are the silver-life bone, or if you have mistaken a shiny coin for that? In Christopher Rey Pérez's first book, everything is wrong and everything is right. What is wrong: you should never heat up your leftover sushi (the speaker does that). Quotidian banalities have taken on forms way beyond food intake lists and masturbation; war, bomb threats and occupied territories are so ordinary as to be background noise. What is right: what this work allows us to see; the ripped, fuzzed-up borders it ekes out, so that we're never exactly sure what country we're walking in (cynic or lyric?). Maybe we've got one foot on one side of the border and one on the other, and maybe there is a wall so we're getting clocked in the crotch as we go, or it's not nations, but no-human's-land we're walking, and the "fuzz" of "fuzzed up" is a mystical cop (and it is always hard to tell what side of the law a mystical cop is on). When I was a kid I saw a cartoon in which an ostrich in a top hat is walking along with one foot on the sidewalk and one foot in the gutter. This makes for an uncomfortable stroll. To fix the situation, s/he ties a knot in the sidewalk poems are kind of like the sidewalk leg and the gutter leg at once, as well as the knot. The knot is also the knot of our era, the work of art in the age of digital reproduction: what is aura? What is art? What is angel? And these poems help us realize that the gnarl now is also the work of art in the age of war reproduction. That the knot of the poem, the thorny place it cannot be undone or reduced or digitized by dominant culture, is not a centralization of power but a diffusion of it; it is the thing that allows us to keep walking this lopsided world.

We find ourselves trying to cross back and forth along the digital/real border. Is this Dante's new limbo, looking for some sonia, some Beatrice, to love or talk to? God will not transcribe everything for us. Master is on one side of the border, Copy on the other. Which real is realer? Can't tell; tie a knot in it and keep walking.

I chose Pérez's work for the Plonsker prize because of this edgy lyric no-human's- land, dark and believing at once. Our angels these days are hyperlinks. Click here to read about Pérez's speakers' angel experiences. No, the links are not broken; they're not even digital, though they're dressed up that way. The links are the poems, our flight paths between here and there.

For other uses, see Angel (disambiguation).
"Angelology" redirects here. For the novel,
see Angelology (novel).

An **angel** is a *supernatural* being or *spirit*
found in various *religions* and *mythologies*.
In *Abrahamic religions* and *Zoroastrianism*,
angels are often depicted as benevolent
celestial beings who act as intermediaries
between God or *Heaven* and *Earth*, or as
guardian spirits or a guiding influence.[1][2]
*Other roles of angels include protecting and
guiding human beings, and carrying out
God's tasks.*[3] *The term "angel" has also
been expanded to various notions of spirits
found in many other religious traditions. The
theological study of angels is known as
"angelology."*

hello on last thursday I was doing laundry and I
removed some clothes from the dryer and looked
down to see if I had dropped any then I went back
to get more clothes when I saw a silvery thing
kinda like a leaf falling I was thinking later
because it wasnt there before and when I tried
to place it in my front pocket in my pink shirt
thats special I couldnt lift it it was heavy like
glue and now Im feeling confused do you think an
angel visits me

Hey, I can say that I've found money when doing the laundry and sometimes my husband's notes he leaves for me with messages like "I <3 you" but I've never seen anything like this silvery thing before.

Can you describe it? Maybe it was an angel and God is watching you.

thanks for a reply right now I dont understand at
all and its making me sick yesterday I throwed
up in the middle of the night ununnounced and it
was wednesday and thats because I was alone and
no one was in the apartment just the mice when I
started to sweat profusely I went back to look at
the thing to analyze it and it wasnt there it had
disappeared just like that and for some reason
I was thinking about the dead people in this
werld and I thinking they really dead or just
pretending because you know some animals pretend
to die and if they do it why not us humans

HI, FIRST OF ALL YOU NEED TO UNDERSTAND THAT HUMANS SHOULD NOT PRETEND TO DIE SO THAT ANGELS CAN VISIT THEM. I KNOW THIS BECAUSE I REALIZED MY OWN ANGELIC HERITAGE IN TIME. I AM A DESCENDENT OF ISRAFIL AND THAT IN ITSELF DEMANDS A SET OF DUTIES. ALL ANGELS HAVE SPECIFIC TASKS THAT THEY MUST PERFORM AND TO FALSELY CALL FORTH AN ANGEL IS TO DEMONSTRATE NEGLECT TOWARD THE DIVINE ECONOMY OF LABOR. AN ANGEL WORKS IN PARTICULAR WAYS AND IT WORKS TOWARD CERTAIN ENDS. ALL METAPHORS FAIL US BUT TRY TO IMAGINE AN ANGEL AS A BEE OR AN ANT OR A SPIDER OR A SNOWFLAKE. IT IS A HAPPENING AND TO MAKE THINGS HAPPEN IS TO ACKNOWLEDGE THE NECESSITY OF WORK. ANGELS WORK AND CALLING FORTH AN ANGEL BY USING DECEPTION PROFILGATES SLOVENLINESS. IT ENCOURAGES DECOMPOSITION. IN A WAY, PRETENDING TO BE DEAD IS ALMOST THE INVERSE OF WHAT IBLEES THOUGHT:

Fire is great and beautiful and better than dirt.
I am made out of fire and Adam is made out of dirt.

∴

It is ignoble of me to bow down before Adam.

SO IN SOME SENSE RETURNING TO, PRETENDING/ FEIGNING, AND THEREBY EXULTING YOUR BASE MATERIALITY IS A GREATER TREACHERY THAN ANYTHING IBLEES COULD EVER THINK OF IN A MILLION HELLS. IT IS HUBRIS. IT IS MONETIZATION OF YOUR OWN DEGRADED WORTH. COWBOY, WE ARE CREATURES THAT MUST PERSIST IN A STATE OF IMPOTENCE. IT IS THE UTOPIA OF NEITHER/ NOR. I THINK THAT WAS GOD'S TRUE GIFT AND IT IS WHAT WE COMMONLY MISTAKE FOR FREE WILL.

আমি ইস্রাফিলরে শিঙ্গার, মহা হুঙ্কার

I want to add my two cents to this thread. Recently, I asked the God if there's a reason for angels and of course I didn't receive a reply. But did Job? Or, in a way that is satisfying, did Abraham? No.

Sometimes we have to wait and that waiting is not to test our patience, which some may think, but to make us suffer. Think about it. There are enough mosquitoes and flies on this planet to drink just a little bit of blood from everyone and shit on all our food. That's why humans don't have wings, and that's why we're made to stand put and wait. When we see silver linings it doesn't necessarily mean they will come to mean anything.

mr cowboy_87,

i did a preliminary "google search" and the only hits for silver thing are rings and coins and in my opinion what you're looking for is neither of those.

keep looking, my best, m.

thanks for the replies people I just want to say
that maybe it was an angel after all because I
was reading the newspaper the day after that day
and everything was in black and white when I was
started thinking is this how I was believing life
like maybe thats why it was a silver thing black
and white mixed in because my heart was really
hurting that moment and I mean it was in pain
like someone was playing with the parts and thats
wrong I said to myself while touching my heart
then and in my pocket in my pink special shirt
there was the silver thing and guess what it had
turned blue the color and now since the morning
Im carrying it everywhere its like a star I
analyzed it it has some sides uneven some of are
pointed and others convex I think if you put it
down on a table it wouldnt stand alone by itself
but Im too scared to try because what if it roll
down away and break

dear cowboy_87,
now those are some cool angels!!!!!!!

Weakestlove wrote:

dear cowboy_87,
now those are some cool angels!!!!!!!

thanks for the reply but whyd you say angels do
you think they are more than one

cowboy_87 wrote:

> Weakestlove wrote:
>
> dear cowboy_87,
> now those are some cool angels!!!!!!!

thanks for the reply but whyd you say angels do you think they are more than one

well, cuz angels like to do things in groups, cowboy_87! go read mat 26: 53: "thinkest thou that I cannot now pray to my father, and he shall presently give me more than twelve legions of angels?" see!!?? and you yourself said the star was silver and now it's blue. that's probably like 2 legions in the very least

men! i've seen an angel on a billboard.
i've seen an angel in a burger king.
i've seen an angel amongst the killing fields.
i've seen an angel wear a cock ring.

comrades! i've seen an angel imitate politicians.
i've seen an angel put away the great martin luther
king
        jr.
i've seen an angel commodify the green marijuana.
i've seen an angel turn his back on our future.

idiots! can it be this is the history of our material song!
dreamers! you joined too and burnt the việt công!

please everyone, i am following this thread close and the
poetry beautiful but i have a similar experience to share and if
you can help me i will appreciate it, i am from the south and
will not say what town because i have to protect my girls but it
is in the north where el chapo wants power, i am a police there
and i know what is the situation with the drugs and immigrants
from america central and i always tried to take care of myself
humbly and my family but sometimes everything you do to live
and be safe and make the good life does not matter in the end
of it. it does not always matter in the end you know and it was
weeks ago when i was to do my tour of the city and of a sudden
a black SUV with four mask men who jumped out sticked a
black bag over my head and push me into the SUV, it was all
of a sudden, i was in the SUV and going somewhere, i do not
know how long the driving was and was thinking about my
daughters at the moment and yes, about my life to. why me, i
wondered, as i said, i am a police and takings happen every day
but i am humble and honest, so why me i was asking until the
SUV stopped then and they take me out and even if i was still
wearing the black bag i can smell the air passed it and realized
we were in the mountains not that far away from my town. a
rifle was pushing me pointed in the back and sits me in a chair
where they tie me up take the bag off and in front i see three
corpses on the floor naked with their heads knifed off. they
were all mexicans, one of them with tattoos one of them with
almost no hairs and short and indian and one of them a woman.
i was looking worried and started breathing with sounds and
the leader kicked me, he knocked me down in the chair i was
tied up to and said, pinche maricón, that is spanich for faggot,
how you to orinate on your self if we not doing anything to
you still. we are treating you good, pinche marrano, and that
is spanich for pig. but i was not hearing any of this because
there was the head of the closest body one meter from my
face on the ground without blood and everything smelled like
cloro like they cleaned up the blood without the bodies and
then put the bodies back for me and that made me have fear

21

when seeing them with the smell of cloro getting me sick, it
was too much, my vision was blurry and inside in the middle
of the neck of the head was something silver, it was like a
shining bone. if i died today they are going to see my silver
thing too? i said to myself. or instead do they know about it?
and is this silver thing speaking for me? is this the thing that
lets us mexicans to cry? i emptied all my thoughts into the
shining bone, i was without no family anymore, no more of my
girls, my parents, i was just breath disappearing as the leader
stepped on my head. vete a la chingada, he said, that is spanich
for go to hell, and he called my name too but my nickname my
compatriots call me and that was more than strange and i will
not say what my nickname is. the whole thing was more than
strange. the other men closed on me then and knifed the ropes
from my wrists and ankles to let me free. they said they were
going to leave the room and that i have to take off my clothes
all of it and run home without looking back and that if i look
back they will shoot me and go home and shoot my daughters
because the police are pigs and the police are not on the side of
the people and the police are extreme cowards and that is why
i was going to run away without looking back because i was a
pig and a coward. then they kick me in the stomach, they step
on my fingers, they slap my face. then they orinate on me, they
squash on my throat, they shoot the gun next to my head. then
they leave and i take off my clothes shaking with the different
kinds of hurt in the brain and the body and was going to leave
but i look back at the silver bone shining, it is shining so bright
and small like a piece of silver from taxco and i say i am
going to take it. i put my hand in the neck of the knifed head,
i remember it was the head of the indian because it was like
one, maybe huichol or yaqui, i do not know, the silver bone
was to attracting to me, the flesh was tough in the neck when i
sticked my fingers in until i grabbed the silver bone with all my
fingers and ripped hard with two hands, one to hold the head
in place and the other to pull and ask if they will see it so i put
it in my mouth and run and leave the ranch and the mountains.

i was running from my soul. i was terrified. i am running for hours under pure desert and night wind and nothing until my feet begin to bleed and i do not stop until my body collapses far from the ranch but still away from town and thirsty. i see a cactus then that was the drinking kind and when i was to drink from it i realized at that moment that i was gasping, the silver bone disappeared or i eated it! then i think maybe it falled out of my mouth when running. then everything black and when i wake up and it was early morning i start walking back to follow my steps and find where i drop the silver bone but i said what if they see me and kill me like they promised? and maybe it was not lost but inside me like i first thinking. i turn around then and go home.

since then, i dream weird. i dream the land is full of aliens and rotting. i try to spend all my time with my daughters. we stay at home and watch cartoons or la selección. and on other days we do puzzles or play the lottery. one day i bring home a dog. when i work, i park my car at the supermarket and wait until i finish my time working around the early evening. i read in inglish. when the words do not make any sense anymore and get tired and turn into spanich i practice porchuguess, i play a game where i am interviewing a beautiful brazil woman who is morena like me and tall with a shining smile. then the game gets me tired and the beautiful woman is speaking spanich not porchuguess and she looks like the girls who leave the chedraui in the hot sun that are sweating down their necks tiny pearls so i say out loud all the words in italien i know like amore, bambini, birra, cane, costo, culo, dolce, dotorre, labbra, libro, ragazza, salvare, and other words and i say them in alphabetical order but eventually i am speaking spanich again, i am always returned to it because the langouges are all very same when romantic and it is still the morning. i do not arrest anyone. i think about the silver bone then and these questions are the ones i write down in my journal:

1. why am i a police and will there be a time i have to kill?

2. really thought i was to die that day or only pretended?

3. ¿if a narco will kill me why god does not kill me first?

4. ¿does god or the angels have to do with that silver bone?

5. ¿was it an adams apple? ¿do women have, it also?

6. ¿is the silver bone tied with sin?

7. is it a secret a message a blessing or a joke?

8. ¿am i a coward like they say?

9. will they come for isabella and montserrat?

10. ¿was it the same voice of my colleague the man that kidnapped me?

Wow, thanks for sharing with us this story. I have chills after that story. Surely the angels blessed you because you are alive today and telling this story.

Thanks for sharing, Vozdehombre. Your English is excellent and I feel privileged to have heard your story.

Click here *to read my experience from 2006.*
Click here *to read my experience from 2009.*
Click here *to read my experience from 2012.*
Click here *to read my other experience from 2012.*
Click here *to read my latest experience (2015).*

VOZDEHOMBRE, WE HAVE TO BREAK THIS
DOWN TO LANGOUGE, WHICH IS WHAT IS SUFFOCATING
YOU WITHOUT A GOD WHO CAN COME PUT A SYNTAX
TO IT. THE SILVER BONE IS PERIPHERAL TO YOU JUST LIKE THE
BLUE STAR IS TO COWBOY_87. GET THAT IN YOUR HEAD!
THINK ABOUT HOW YOU FEEL FIRST AND HOW THESE
FEELINGS MAKE YOU FEEL. YOU NEED MAYBE A THOUSAND
MORE QUESTIONS TO UNDERSTAND WHAT HAPPENED TO
YOU. WHEN ANGELS REACH OUT TO US THEY ARE TRANS-
GRESSING CHAINS OF CAUSALITY SO THAT WE DO NOT
HAVE TO TRAVEL SUCH LONG DISTANCES. THEY ARE DOING
OUR WORK. EVEN SO, GOD WILL NOT TRANSCRIBE EVERY-
THING FOR US. THIS IS SOMETHING WE MUST DO OUR-
SELVES.

আমি ইস্রাফিলের শিঙ্গার, মহা হুঙ্কার

Vozdehombre wrote:

please everyone, i am following this thread close and the poetry beautiful but i have a similar experience to share and if you can help me i will appreciate it, i am from the south and will not say what town because i have to protect my girls but it is in the north where el chapo wants power, i am a police there and i know what is the situation with the drugs and immigrants from america central and i always tried to take care of myself humbly and my family but sometimes everything you do to live and be safe and make the good life does not matter in the end of it. it does not always matter in the end you know and it was weeks ago when i was to do my tour of the city and of a sudden a black SUV with four mask men who jumped out sticked a black bag over my head and push me into the SUV, it was all of a sudden, i was in the SUV and going somewhere, i do not know how long the driving was and was thinking about my daughters at the moment and yes, about my life to. why me, i wondered, as i said, i am a police and takings happen every day but i am humble and honest, so why me i was asking until the SUV stopped then and they take me out and even if i was still wearing the black bag i can smell the air passed it and realized we were in the mountains not that far away from my town. a rifle was pushing me pointed in the back and sits me in a chair where they tie me up take the bag off and in front i see three corpses on the floor naked with their heads knifed off. they were all mexicans, one of them with tattoos one of them with almost no hairs and short and indian and one of them a woman. i was looking worried and started breathing with sounds and the leader kicked me, he knocked me down in the chair i was tied up to and said, pinche maricón, that is spanich for faggot, how you to orinate on your self if we not doing anything to you still. we are treating you good, pinche marrano, and that is spanich for pig. but i was not hearing any of this because there was the head of the closest body one meter from my face on the ground without blood and everything smelled like cloro like they cleaned up the blood without the bodies and then put the bodies back for me and that made me have fear when seeing them with the smell of cloro getting me sick, it was too much, my vision was blurry and inside in the middle of the neck of the head was something silver, it was like a shining bone. if i died today they are going to see my silver thing too? i said to myself. or instead do they know about it? and is this silver thing speaking for me? is this the thing that lets us mexicans to cry? i emptied all my thoughts into the shining bone, i was without no family anymore, no more of my girls, my parents, i was just breath disappearing as the leader stepped on my head. vete a la chingada, he said, that is spanich for go to hell, and he called my name too but my nickname my compatriots call me and that was more than strange and i will not say what my nickname is. the whole thing was more than strange. the other men closed on me then and knifed the ropes from my wrists and ankles to let me free. they said they were going to leave the room and that i have to take off my clothes all of it and run home without looking back and that if i look back they will shoot me and go home and shoot my daughters because the police are pigs and the police are not on the side of the people and the police are extreme cowards and that is why i was going to run away without looking back because i was a pig and a coward. then they kick me in the stomach, they step on my fingers, they slap my face. then they orinate on me, they squash on my throat, they shoot the gun next to my head. then they leave and i take off my clothes shaking with the different kinds of hurt in the brain and the body and was going to leave but i look back at the silver bone shining, it is shining so bright and small like a piece of silver from taxco and i say i am going to take it. i put my hand in the neck of the knifed head, i remember it was the head of the indian because it was like one, maybe huichol or yaqui, i do not know, the silver bone was to attracting to me, the flesh was tough in the neck when i sticked my fingers in until i grabbed the silver bone with all my fingers and ripped hard with two hands, one to hold the head in place and the other to pull and ask if they will see it so i put it in my mouth and run and leave the ranch and the mountains. i was running from my soul. i was terrified. i am running for hours under pure desert and night wind and nothing until my feet begin to bleed and i do not stop until my body collapses far from the ranch but still away from town and thirsty. i see a cactus then that was the drinking kind and when i was to drink from it i realized at that moment that i was gasping, the silver bone disappeared or i eated it! then i think maybe it falled out of my mouth when running. then everything black and when i wake up and it was early morning i start walking back to follow my steps and find where i drop the silver bone but i said what if they see me and kill me like they promised? and maybe it was not lost but inside me like i first thinking. i turn around then and go home.

since then, i dream weird. i dream the land is full of aliens and rotting. i try to spend all my time with my daughters. we stay at home and watch cartoons or la selección. and on other days we do puzzles or play the lottery. one day i bring home a dog. when i work, i park my car at the supermarket and wait until i finish my time working around the early evening. i read in inglish. when the words do not make any sense anymore and get tired and turn into spanich i practice porchuguess, i play a game where i am interviewing a beautiful brazil woman who is morena like me and tall with a shining smile. then the game gets me tired and the beautiful woman is speaking spanich not porchuguess and she looks like the girls who leave the chedraui in the hot sun that are sweating down their necks tiny pearls so i say out loud all the words in italien i know like amore, bambini, birra, cane, costo, culo, dolce, dotorre, labbra, libro, ragazza, salvare, and other words and i say them in alphabetical order but eventually i am speaking spanich again, i am always returned to it because the langouges are all very same when romantic and it is still the morning.

i do not arrest anyone. i think about the silver bone then and these questions are the ones i write down in my journal:

1. ¿why am i a police and will there be a time i have to kill?

2. ¿i really thought i was to die that day or only pretended?

3. ¿if a narco will kill me why god does not kill me first?

4. ¿does god or the angels have to do with that silver bone?

5. ¿was it an adams apple? ¿do women have, it also?

6. ¿is the silver bone tied with sin?

7. ¿is it a secret a message a blessing or a joke?

8. ¿am i a coward like they say?

9. ¿will they come for isabella and montserrat?

10. ¿was it the same voice of my colleague the man that kidnapped me?

kompa t mereses una salida komo los demas de este pinshe infierno kabron. nadie debe bibir en este desmadre pinshe jodido del pri. x eso nos enkontramos kon angeles ya k aki no ay diablos sino muertos. yo kruse ase kuatro a˜os mejor kosa k ise jamas. aorita tengo una linda morra y estoi jalando en los angeles. gano shingon karnal. mira buskate un koyote no mas bas a tener k aorrar shingos komo 5 mil al menos pero te ba a baler madre kuando ya estes instalado aki kon un buen jale t juro

I d like to join this forum because of an uncanny event that happened to me which I ll now recount.

When my girlfriend and I hav sex I ask her to choke me. The practice s called erotic asphyxiation and in fact it s not so uncommon.several studies
find that anywhere from six to nine percent of couples practice some kind of breath control play during coitus. At first my girlfriend didn t enjoy the fact I m a gasper but now it s the de facto coefficent for multiplying our pleasure.

This all changed a few weeks ago thouh.when we were at my flat and I accidentally fainted.
I m unsure of the length of time I was gone when I came to I had a bloody hand towel lying on my chest and my girlfriend was sitting on the floor completely distraugt or perhaps I read into her wrongly I must admit that I was not im my full capacity to assess myself much less other people.

I still felt very light-headed and despite the bloody hand towel there were no visible injuries to my [erson.
the entire roomed seemed strange.
As it were composed of different proportions in an impossible space and my girlfriend looked so harmless and wrong in thisd space.
It occurred to me to ask her if she was fine.
She she had almost killed me.
She said this so matterof factly that I felt afraid for her.
my girlfriend said while mounted on you I felt somethinf in your throat I wanted to squeeze and force into your heart
The desire was stronger than my desire for you. It was like math(We are both studying)Or some other pleasurable abstraction of a higher plane.

I asked her to describe the object she felt in my throat then
and when she responded with a many pointed star I asked
her do you mean a dodecahjedron.
And if it was a dodecahedron I aske,d. Was it a
greatstellated dodecahedron? Or a concave pyritohedral
dodecahedron?or was it even a dodecahedron I wanted to
know.
Perhaps it was another kind of kepler poinsot polyjhedron
like a great icosahedron or maybe it wasnt a keplerpoinsot
at all

You know at times like these it s necessary to be as
specific as possible and by that I mean it s necessary for us
to scientific and precise with each other
I said with a fake smile I was tryin to muster.
My girlfriend couldn t answer though. She said I squeezed
anf squeezed until I wanted you dead.

...I think the star was silver

It s been four days since this event and I haven t seen my
girlfriend since then.
What s this silver object and why does she think that it
wads silver.
I normally would proceed through the standard sequence
of scientific inquiry to reach a conclusion that s within an
acceptable margin of error but Iam not that dense
as to think our physical reality s not susceptible to
noomena we ve yet the ability to classify.the appearance of
the bloody hand towel for instance.

It s possiblethis star doen t follow our current
understanding of the laws of geometry
and it s also possible something holy or at least celestial or
at the very least supermatural   entirely outside the laws of
geometry may have inhabited me I don t know

This is why I need to enlist your helpI think I m different

I find pleasure in simple things now and despite my
problems wit girlfriend I feel closer to people.
I want to determine the cause of these occurrences. I m
normally aloof person.
Cowboy will you please describe the physical dimensions
of the blue star as well as upload several high res pics of it
from different angles onto imgur? and vozdehombre
once cowbou does this.will you confirm whether the
shining bone was similarly shaped?

Thank you.

excuse me, i want to say that you all must be very careful to distinguish between good and evil, between kind-acts and theater. it's probable that evil angels visited you all. just look around. there're evil angels everything. there're websites (www.xvideos.com/.../israeli_army_girls_fuck_sex_2010_700mb_dvdrip). there're hollywood films (https://en.wikipedia.org/wiki/The_Exterminating_Angel_(film)). there're hotlines (http://www.angelshotline.com/prices/). angels don't do choking! no matter what the scripture says. when you touch an angel down there all there is is something like gesso and that's the way it should be.

hypotenoose, I have a urgent question for you. your girlfriend is sonia? please call me +972 (056) 939 – 4121 we need to talk and I am going

bump

My life is my message. —Mahatami Ghandi

thanks for all the reply I was gone for some time
because I was very sad I was going to the store
to buy some things I needed for the residence and
was walking with my hand on my chest pocket in my
special pink shirt to protect the blue star un-
til I was in the store and this is what I bought
two gallons of milk some cans of peas a couple of
ramen and toothbrush and when I paid the monei-
es it suddenly made sense that I had to carry
these things with two hands so I tried putting
everything in one bag but it tore and made a mess
everything was spilled everywhere on the count-
er we had to rebag the items and I thought about
putting the blue star in the bag too then but I
didnt want the milk to accidentally crush it con-
sidering it was heavy milk so I gave up and car-
ried the bags home with two hands and when I got
home the blue star was gone from my chest pocket
in my special pink shirt like I imagined and when
I went back to the store to see if I had dropped
it then well not there so I went along the street
and not there either it was useless these days
and nights in bed all by myself there is noth-
ing for me anymore and if it was an angel that
was with me it was an angel evil and extreme just
like you said it was evil it was evil because it
only brought happiness when it was around and
sadness when it was not and that is evil dont you
agree what kind of life is that tell me because
Im trying to look on the bright side but its so
hard I say what if the blue star left me to guard
vozdehombre and maybe I was going to die instead
of pretending to like the animals and now that it
left me that means Im not going to die anymore is
what I mean like the risk gone now or something I
dont know what do you guys think Im having weird
dreams too like vozdehombre

dear cowbow_87,
there are legions!!!!!!

Weakestlove wrote:

dear cowboy_87,
there are legions!!!!!!!!

thanks weakestlove but I need more answers

Not devoid of feeling.

DR. MARTIN HORACIO VARGAS CHIMALPOPOCA

UNIVERSIDAD NACIONAL AUTÓNOMA DE MÉXICO   CED. PROF. 1584290

MÉDICO CIRUJANO

Nombre del Paciente: REY

Fecha:

TA: (CC-fc)

F.C.: 76

F.R.: 27 C

TEMP.: _____

PESO: _____

TALLA: _____

I.D.: fascia fisura pie izq

EDAD: 27 c

1) Vitamina B con Diclofenaco I inyección tab.
   I. Muscular IC 2 ampolletas

2) Naproxeno tabletas 500 mg
   1C / 8 hrs x 5 dias (C/ comida)

3) Acidam Citofexista en casa te
   40 mg ficación con el tratamiento
   de establecta.

Tempest, the Furious Winds, an(are intermediate between
follows these. ngs and defend the rights
   *And the source of these spirits is*nst the usurpations of the
Messengers are sent.

But Tehura admits that these relat(them was born Tii.
The most orthodox classification*Desire*), and of them were
The Gods are divided into Atuas(senger of shadows and of
The superior Atuas are all sons a(enger of light and of life;
They dwell in the heavens. Th of the things of heaven;
Taaroa and his wife Feii Feii Maïte(he things of the earth.
first of the gods after his father, and w(of the within who watches
Tetaï Mati and Oüroü Tetefa), Raae without who guards the
Oüroü, Feoïto, Teheme, Roa Roa(f the sands, and Tii of the
Temoüria), Tané (father of Peüroïth, Tii of the rocks and Tii
of the solid earth.' endowed with an instinctive feel
   Still later were boi(ry between human creations a(ht, the
happenings of the da reflux,
the giving and receiv(

The images of the i(nds of
the *maraës* (temples)((rcum-
scribed the sacred pla(rea(important circumstances. on
the sea-shores. These(a tree, for example, as, (king the
boundaries between t(ter he attribute(divine ((ning the
balance between the (out apparent((ng their
reciprocal encroach(re conjecture((ve seen a
few statues of Tiis o(colossal
outlines partaking o(nd bear
witness to a special c(ine skill
in the art of working(cturally
constructed of super(and in-
genious combination(

The European inv(stroyed
these vestiges of a civ(ndeur.
When the Tahitians (achieve
miracles of bad taste— (omare.
They had been richly ((ing for
the harmony necessa(nd the

Change of residence.

```
itxwasx19:47xthenxandxaxb
outxofxaxshopxtoxwashxthe
intoxhisxjacketxandxtookx
andxwatchingxhimxwithxhis
hisxleftxhandxwhilwxwipin          hisxoverallsxcomex
withxhisxrightxthenxswitc          owsxandxreachingx
andxswitchingxtoxhisxrigh          nguichxatt19:48x
leftxbeforexswitchingxitx          ngxsanguichxinx
xleftxagainxatx19:49xandx          windowsxcleanedx
gettingxparanoidxhexmight          txdownxthexragx
stinexthenxixlisteningxcl          praixwithxhisx
increasingxbeforexfeeling          xfuckingxsanguich
thexworkersxwaixitxwent            isperingxthenxix
                                   lkingxaboutxpale
                                   thenxmixparanoiax
"eexfuexasixunxpoquitoxex          evedxhexsangxinx
llegoxeexquexvoixaxhacerx
eexgeaciasxaxellaxconocix
asixloxquexcomenzoxenxuna
laxleccionxquexsexllevoxm          xlaxmaneraxenxquex
creiaxenxesasxcosasxdexam          roboxmixcorazonx
comproboxquexpalxamorxnox          exesxamorxeexfuex
                                   xdexpasionxvaiax
andxthexsongxwasxnicexfuc          azonxpuesxlloxnox
inalxshitlutionsxofxthexq          xunaxvezxmasxsex
sawxaxcorpsexcomingxtoxth          excondicion"
ixsawxaxdiabolicalxmirror
wasx19:fiftee-onexthexboj          hooughxthexlibid-
dxhurreexupxorxnotxworkin          exitxwasx19:49xix
xoldxmanxfatxreturnedxtox          acexatx19:fiftee
xchildrenxfuckingxexiting          axtearxthenxitx
womenxholdingxhandsxenter          sxcomexoutxandxsai
ileexwithxaxchiuahuaxpas           txenoughxthenxthis
toxenterxthexstorexbutxt           torexandxsomexlopd
xsaidxno                           storexandxtwox
                                   exstorexbhenxaxfaa
                                   xandxitxwantingx
                                   herxofxthexfamilee
```

Angels for everybody.

animal and plant life

rat██ ██ █████ ████████
conta██ ███ ██, ███
"savages," ██ ███ █████
thi█ █████ They █████
masterpieces, but █████
have become █████████

█████ the fourth █
██████ ████ meters, ██
decorated this ██████

The █████ had an
spec███████ ██ █████
gre████████ ███ ███
invo████ ███ █████
But her ████
negative ████ █████

Such texts would █
██ ████ Bible co███
tary, T██ ████
ligion based ██ ███
█████████ ███ █████
n█████ of M█████ █
diff█████ █████████
██████████
interesting and sing█
I should like to poi█
indicate them. Th██
matter for savants.
It is █████ █████
univers█ princip█

xtant place in the me

```
marx
xxxxxxxxxxxxxxxxxxxxxisxbutxhistorees
xxxxxxxxxxxxxxxxxxxxxxxxxxxxcorner
```

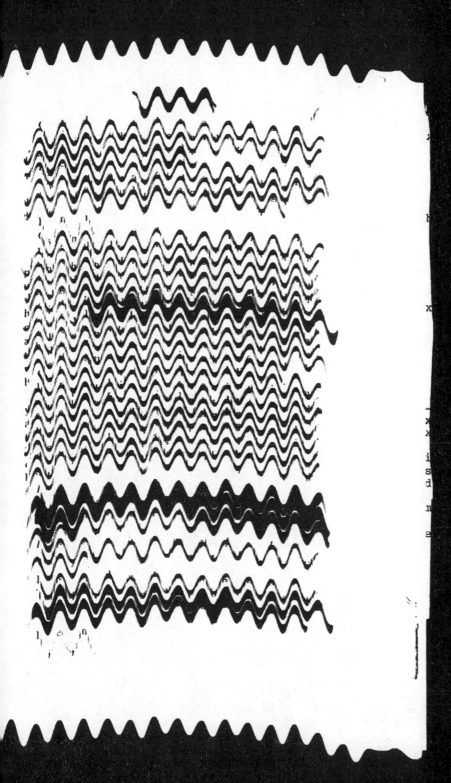

furrows in

only for
my per-
thing that

in her
journey
to the

drove me
I was

began.
radiant
of our
She no
longer
to her of

nt in the
the firs

lights!
docile
on o...
I mig...
uld h...
her...

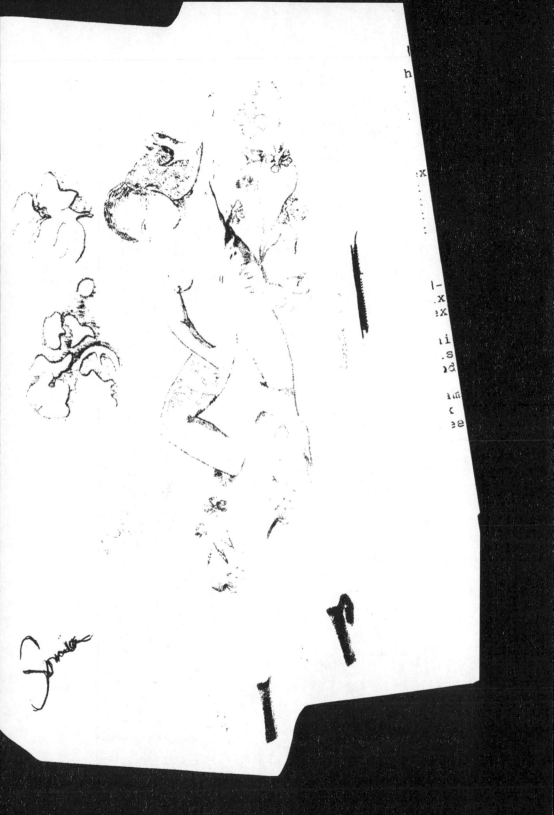

The wings are heavy. The whole thing is print

Tahiti will die, it will die never to rise again.

he might found with her among the most
experienced and favored, above all the others, ... of men a race
Peïa, a high mountain on the island .... descended upon
dwelt his sisters, the goddesses Te......

Oro, transformed into a young warri....... Bora, ...se
young girls set out upon a journey ....ation ....
find them the venture descending of the .... the island, he

Oro ....

.... of a god.

In the different isles where people .... the god
fair and magnificent visitors, they ....
feasts to which all the women flocked.

And Oro gazed upon them.

But his heart was filled with sad......
love, but he did not love. His glance .... the god found
find the virtues and graces of which .... not remain long

And after many days had been cons......
decided to return to heaven, where he .... again such, he
island of Bora Bora, on ....side of ......
little valley of .... village on the

S....
a....
le....

Enchanted, Oro pr.... his sister..... .... girl for him.

He ....rein ... to speak to the young
o........

The goddesses in approaching the .... the ....
her, praised her beauty, and told h....
Ava..........., Bora Bora ....

"O.... the other asks of you whethe.......... .... from
become his wife."

Va.......................... will ....
scrutinized .... carefully

"You are not from. Ave..."

ibxwasx17:32xandxrubbingx
bodeexandxsittingxalonexi
spacexandxnoticingxtherex
gxgringoxspacexthexrexwasx
xtherexwasxmonkeiesxtooxa
xforxpinchexfuckxsakexitx
ticxvinesxandxgreenxsmoot
llogurtsxixwasxhavingxtox
habitatxixwasxworkingxint
mixpegxlegxhoppingxalongx
xhatxwasxwrappedxonxmexbo
fashionxitxwasx17fifteefi
xgulpxixmeanxitxwasx17:3s
ingxextremexpurgexixwasxn
itxwasx17:37xitxwasx17:38
andxixwasxallxoutxofxvita
axnailsclipperxixemanated
tingxmixhormonesxthenxixw
ateleexnailxintoxitxitxwa
xandxthexeconomeexisxbadx
ionxdownx17xpereentxandxt
toxexportxandxwexnotxhave
processxitxinflationxbein
andx27xmorexdiextodaixinx
niansxsheekingxshelterxin
thexdamagexinflictingxwas
xandxbackxherexitxwasxsep
43xstudentsxmissingxandxi
thinkingxaboutxallxthatxa
xsomexthinkingxbecausexit
fuckedxupxtoxthinkingxixe
courtiersxfingerxwhencext
gatherxmilkxforxtheirxwor
itxwasx17:41xandxixwasxio
xairxixcouldntxbelievexth
oningxairxitxwasxtoxbecom
txoutxofxthexfuckingxairx
xbackxtoxpalestinexwherex
axpoemxandxdeenaxwasxshow
herxbeautifulxbabeexafte
xtakingxpicturesxofxbanks
amirxwasxdrawingxgoruxan
readingxaxbookxwhilextal
hebaxandnaghamxwasxspeak
chxandxmohammadxwasxspea
xandx xuthmanxwasxspeaking
andxnasreexwasxspeakingx
shxandxlaithx wasxspeakin

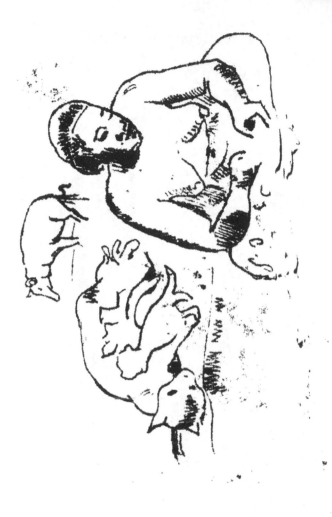

At home.

01.05.15. make run for milk, eggs, vegetable oil, toothpaste, anchovies, then post office, seven 2X4s, red socks, and coffee. don't forget staple gun. sweet talk waste management. yesterday was uneventful and bacchanal. the little brass bell going off. medieval autodidactic utopias. good dog food I couldn't digest.

02.05.15. my kidneys like these new antibiotics. did I see sonia at the GYM? thinking of gauguin in réunion. why?

03.05.15. ransack the chicken coop. masturbate today. in the afternoon a cop was annihilated. at sundown master texting with 💀

04.05.15. I want the love heart soul thinking.

05.05.15. what's happening yesterday? was an accumulation of? the students say another one needs letter of rec to study in germany. comfort even in austerity. it's cinco de mayo. ontological profiteers of time. I heat the sushi.

06.05.15. sweater goes folded in the black milk crate. simulacral fling was a not sonia. but that given. later I sleep through brief and haunted periods. everything expressed into crud. drugs.

07.05.15. I have inconstant
habits. gas is $2.45 cents
now. remember to dry out
the TARPAULIN. arabic at
9 tonight.

08.05.15. today was really hymnal!

09.05.15. sugars bad for candida overgrowth (*Candida Albicans is a normally harmless yeast infection found in the mouth, intestinal tract, and vagina*). look up "pau d'arco" and "caprylic acid." // they almost evicting the local accent but I'm here and reading gauguin had a lover in tahiti, not réunion (wikipedia). spent all morning on google to find out named "tehura." and well I think his reds are the best. his greens are weird green european. also reading him being dubbed "ta-ata vahine" (man-woman).

10.05.15. happiness and expatiation) xerox grade of reading. saturdays are for heaving into it.

11.05.15. it's flooding and 2pm. weather girl talking about tropical storm "sonya." six inches; almost seven. aren't we in summer? I feel like a giant worm that eats green things without knowing the beauty of what green things can be. now without reason it's may. "enhancing my prison features."

12.05.15. master texted with the word "apúrate" but how? hurried with the trimming of mustache-(gone). hurried with the weighted crunches-(done). (hurried with the milking-weaned). hurried with the testing-(creeping).

13.05.15. publicity stunt failure with the second cop. in effect, something due to "pinches gabachos culeros" and power, something over fucking "it" with firearms. // saw a ladybug today. also saw bird with red under the belly carry worm toward palm trees.

14.05.15. cracked a teeth. thinking of sonia incessantly feel like gut emptied.

15.05.15. can't sleep. thinking about how sweat accretes. // banda is cursilería + teatro griego. corridos are alfabetización + revolución x la muerte. conjunto is golosinas + vaqueros − lo agresivo. rancheras are tristeza + el vacío ÷ la historia + la época de oro del cine + gritos. tejano is sintetizador + selena + f-250s + la economía del dólar.

16.05.15. yesterday was un-american but at the same time typically american in some ways. I separate the colors for the wash. they extolled the virtues of long legs and white skin. I like thick legs and dark skin.

17.05.15. years behind everything. ordered "noa noa" notebook online ($5.95 dover fine art) and "social behavior in farm animals" ($17.80 CABI publishing). // what if name were cabeza de vaca? empress carlota? or malinche? benito pablo juárez garcía? motecuhzoma xocoyotzin (or alternately, montezuma, moteuczoma, or moctezuma ii)? doesn't matter anyways if they won't call me rey. it's night now. could smash the mosquitoes and try to sleep. how I got here?

18.05.15. lanyard got catched on motorcycle. my right foot broke. saw an angel with braided hair. it whispering something about incorrigible love. my blood dilated. I passing out. panting. then waking up in bed.

19.05.15. hospital bill in dollars. thinking about returning to abu dis. tomb of lazarus or langouge or tear gas and that's life and that's tough or so they say while safely away. but, why was *that* dilation yesterday so steroidal? where does the coda go after imposed evil? I hop to the walgreens and schemed.

20.05.15. got a new alum block. prioritizing "on agglutination," "on the body in aztec space," "on christ jrs" in order to understand the parts. arnica not working but still effecting a more efficient limp. also, I find a tattoo on my heel. don't remember a thing. the angel was a not sonia.

21.05.15. arabic tonight at
9. today: unliving continuity.

22.05.15. I drink red wine.
I dipping finger into. sonia
I am still here. hello I am
straight ahead. sonia I am
writing and straight ahead.

23.05.15. dreamed the angel came back to pet me. both feet were broke. the broke one a lot of and the unbroke one broke but not as much as broke one right now. good for a hobble I thinking but on my back with sores. visions and ranch life. drawing blood from the well. we with pearl snap buttons. eventually I sweating everything up when each question come. then I unbraiding its hair before all the protein gone.

24.05.15. bed to outhouse with limp: 13 seconds. bed to outhouse with adjusted limp: 9 seconds. bed to kitchen with limp: 20 seconds. bed to kitchen with adjusted limp: 17 seconds. // this morning the angel denied *cops rhymes with mops.*

25.05.15. as a mythical series of conceptions I found myself elevated.

26.05.15. do angels get dirty? are angels clean? do angels attract parasites? was there angels at the beating? can angels do sonia? must they obey DHT? will they ferment my bread? why they taste like petrol? how they go like a storm? why they have french-braided hair?

27.05.15. gauguin arrived. reproductions low quality sucks. can't read today because master texting with "repeat guagüis." (gauguin / guagüis!?) also, my song play twice on the radio: *la chica que soñé — tropical panama.*

28.05.15. thinking about getting on a forum about what happened. my foot is turned silver. am I more than mourning. I feel like excessing. I feel like a recycled body. // "noa noa" library of congress info: Gauguin, Paul, 1848-1903 // Noa Noa : the Tahitian journal. /// Translated from the French. // Reprint. Originally published: New York : N.L. Brown, 1920, c1919. // 1. Gauguin, Paul, 1848-1903. 2. Painters—France—Biography. 3. Tahiti I. Title. // ND553. G27A2 1985 759.4 [B] 84-21058 // ISBN-13: 978-0-486-24859-2 // ISBN-10: 0-486-24859-3

29.05.15. student wrote saying misses me. she will become a doctor. the jaish were on campus ground again and shooting. my foot is shrinking. new plan max out as many credit cards as I'm offered.

30.05.15. looking high up and the skull gets fracked. buy yogurts. check on the pigs and ducks and goats. it looks like it's going to get to happen even if belated and humid. so I work in haste and not dispassionately.

31.05.20. found this on page 17: *Even after this long time I still take pleasure in remembering the TRUE and REAL emotions in this TRUE and REAL nature.*

2015-06-02 18:46:23	Detail	United States	Jacksonville, FL
2015-06-02 18:31:14	Detail	United States	Fargo, ND
2015-06-02 17:51:15	Detail	Afghanistan	Ghazni
2015-06-02 17:47:20	Detail	Afghanistan	Kandahar
2015-06-02 17:19:53	Detail	United States	Milwaukie, OR
2015-06-02 16:21:34	Detail	India	Bijapur
2015-06-02 15:54:00	Detail	Iraq	Ramadi
2015-06-02 15:51:00	Detail	Iraq	Tuz Khurmato
2015-06-02 15:42:23	Detail	United States	Morgan County, IN
2015-06-02 15:05:40	Detail	Palestinian Territory	Sheikh, Radwah
2015-06-02 15:02:39	Detail	United States	Union City, CA
2015-06-02 14:59:17	Detail	United States	Pittsburgh, PA
2015-06-02 14:49:00	Detail	United States	Santa Maria, CA
2015-06-02 14:13:00	Detail	United States	Oklahoma City, OK
2015-06-02 13:38:44	Detail	India	South Garo Hills

FLORIDA - Regency Mall Evacuated - JSO Investigating

NORTH DAKOTA - Bomb Threat Reported At West Acres Mall

AFGHANISTAN - ANP Discovered And Neutralized 6 Mines

AFGHANISTAN - 2 Terrorists Arrested In Kandahar - Hand Grenades Recovered

OREGON - Bomb Threat In Roseburg Ends With Arrest

INDIA - Woman Naxal Killed In Gun-Fight With Security Forces In Chhattisgarh - Hand Grenades Seized

IRAQ - Federal Police Attack ISIS By Artillery Shells In Response On Targeting 1 Of Their Barracks

IRAQ - Kurdish Islamist Partys Headquarters Exposed To An Armed Attack In Tuz Khurmato

INDIANA - Suspicious Package Brings Bomb Squad To County

GAZA - Gunman Killed In Clashes With Hamas Security In Gaza City

CALIFORNIA - Bomb Squad Investigates Suspicious Device At Adult School

PENNSYLVANIA - Bomb Squad Called To Brighton Heights After Discovery Of Possible Live Mortar

CALIFORNIA - Explosive Found In Santa Maria Home

OKLAHOMA - Man Arrested After Claiming Device In Backpack Was Grenade

INDIA - GNLA Ultra Held - Bomb Disposal Squad Called

2015-06-02 13:36:00	Detail	United States	Hermitage, PA
2015-06-02 13:29:15	Detail	Iraq	Baiji
2015-06-02 12:57:00	Detail	Mexico	McAllen
2015-06-02 11:56:41	Detail	United States	Augusta, ME
2015-06-02 11:54:01	Detail	United States	Ohare International Airport, IL
2015-06-02 11:21:29	Detail	United States	Hartsfield-Jackson Atlanta International Airport
2015-06-02 10:55:36	Detail	Iraq	Baghdad
2015-06-02 10:31:00	Detail	Thailand	Bangkok
2015-06-02 10:00:00	Detail	United States	Jacksonville, FL
2015-06-02 09:45:47	Detail	Nigeria	Maiduguri
2015-06-02 08:47:00	Detail	India	Koraput
2015-06-02 08:39:00	Detail	Nigeria	Maiduguri
2015-06-02 08:08:41	Detail	United States	Philadelphia International Airport, PA
2015-06-02 07:27:00	Detail	Mexico	Matamoros
2015-06-02 07:14:00	Detail	United States	Guadalajara International Airport

PENNSYLVANIA - Police Investigating Hermitage Wal-Mart Fire

IRAQ - 28 Militiamen Killed In Car Bombings In Iraq

MEXICO - Feds Uncover Black Market For Grenades In Texas Near Border

MAINE - Cony HS Evacuated After Reported Bomb Threat

ILLINOIS - Law Enforcement Official Says Airline Bomb Threats Not Credible

GEORGIA - Atlanta - Bomb Threats Made Against Five Airliners

IRAQ - 4 Killed in Car Bomb Attack In Iraqs Baghdad

THAILAND - Sriwara Orders Inquiry Into Bombs Found In Parking Space

FLORIDA - No Devices Found After Regency Square Mall Received Bomb Threat Calls

NIGERIA - Bomb Blast Hits Market In Maiduguri City - 50 Killed

INDIA - Landmine Blast - Narrow Escape For BSF Men

NIGERIA - Boko Haram Launches Fresh Attack On NE Nigerian City

PENNSYLVANIA - San Diego-based Flight Evacuated In Philadelphia After Bomb Threat Hoax

MEXICO - 4 People Wounded In Bomb Attack In Matamoros

MEXICO - Multiple Hoax Threats Against US Aircraft

2015-06-02 06:43:00	Detail	United States	San Francisco International Airport, CA
2015-06-02 06:29:00	Detail	United States	Germantown, TN
2015-06-02 05:32:11	Detail	Afghanistan	Sharana
2015-06-02 04:28:19	Detail	Afghanistan	Kandahar
2015-06-02 04:12:12	Detail	Uganda	Katakwi
2015-06-02 04:07:26	Detail	Bulgaria	Sofia
2015-06-02 02:06:00	Detail	United States	Roseburg, OR
2015-06-02 01:52:00	Detail	United States	Neenah, WI
2015-06-02 01:44:00	Detail	Thailand	Yannawa
2015-06-02 01:39:00	Detail	United States	Lompoc, CA
2015-06-02 00:37:00	Detail	Iraq	Baghdad
2015-06-02 00:35:00	Detail	United States	Concord, NH
2015-06-02 00:30:00	Detail	Iraq	Mosul
2015-06-02 00:21:00	Detail	Iraq	Falasteen
2015-06-02 00:16:00	Detail	Iraq	Tikrit

CALIFORNIA - Flight Lands Safely At San Francisco International Airport After International Security

TENNESSEE - Grenade Found In Germantown Trash Can

AFGHANISTAN - Afghan Police Shot Dead 2 Would-be Suicide Bombers

AFGHANISTAN - 2 Terrorists Arrested In Kandahar

UGANDA - Grenade Kills 2 In Katakwi District

BULGARIA - Bomb Signal At Bulgarias National Radio

OREGON - Man Threatens To Blow Self Up - Mobile Home Park Evacuated

WISCONSIN - Neenah Police Investigate Works Bombs Near City Hall

THAILAND - Arms Cache Found In Tourist Boat Links To A Retired Senior Thai Navy Officer

CALIFORNIA - Police Investigating Pressure Cooker Left Outside Lompoc Walgreens

IRAQ - 3 Traffic Police Wounded In A Roadside Bomb In Baghdad

NEW HAMPSHIRE - Bomb Threat Reported At The Steeplegate Mall

IRAQ - ISIS Blow Up 8 Houses Belonging To Christian In Mosul

IRAQ - Car Bomb Explosion Near A Restaurant Killed 2 Wounded 8 In Baghdad

IRAQ - Suicide Truck Bomber Destroyed In Tikrit

01.06.15.   found   this
on page 19: *With the*
suppleness of an animal
and the graceful litheness
of an androgyne he walked
a few paces in advance of
me. And it seemed to me
that I saw incarnated in
him, palpitating and living,
all the magnificent plant-
life which surrounded us.
From it in him, through him
there became disengaged
and emanated a powerful
perfume of beauty. Was
it really a human being
walking there ahead of
me? Was it the naïve
friend by whose combined
simplicity and complexity
I had been so attracted?
Was it not rather the
Forest itself, the living
Forest, without sex—and
yet alluring?

02.06.15. angel was plant life or some habitat of? // to his credit gauguin learning the langouge (it was probably not gauguin). "the living forest..." yeah. —"THE LIVING FOREST."

03.06.15. my foot a hard sharp point I stab steaks with. $4.99/lb. yesterday my cousin caught by ATF. (1) being here and only here is predicated on the structure being sutured. (2) reading is frightening and dangerous. (3) I'm Tahiti. (4) I want to forget the angel. (5) I'm not safe inside the appearance of whitened generosity. (6) BLACK OUT EVERYTHING. (7) it was in coordination with the gulf cartel. (8) all this is very likely.

04.06.15. make run for eggs, milk, alfalfa, anchovies, maseca, beef tips, industrial detergent, valerian root, trump piñata, WD-40, corn nuts, lice shampoo, and leftover plywood. hey, I saw more than 7 children today! they were all swimming in a canal hurt happy with stray dogs. then thinking about gauguin again. mainly fucked up.

05.06.15. is there more comprehensive concepts for "sonia," "the angel," "tehura"? "nature"? like a kind of subterfuge? I think noa noa either means fragrance or rosewood) get further instructions from master. today is my "birthday."

06.06.15. dreamed of an orgy with four sonias. later, a green carpet, a trident, a package of packing noodles, solar panels on my coffin, a hurricane, silicone buttplugs shaped like lizards, and fields of yellow corn.

07.06.15. on page 43: The wings are heavy. The whole thing is primitive. ??!!??!?!?!

08.06.15. my pointed foot turning silver. upped my lecithin intake. called ernesto today and he says armadillos carry leprosy. dolphins have more sophisticated langouge-uses than humans. time to evacuate. medical bills coming.

09.06.15. cop got acquitted. master texting with lyrics: *UNA KRUS DE MADERA DE LA MAS KORRIENTE ♫ ESO ES LO KE PIDO KUANDO YO ME MUERA ♫ YO NO KIERO LUJOS KE BALGAN MIYONES ♫ LO UNIKO KE KIERO ES KE TOKEN KANSIONES ♫ KE SE AGA UNA FIESTA LA MUERTE DE UN POVRE ♫ YO NO KIERO SHANTOS ♫ NO KIERO TRISTESAS ♫ YO NO KIERO PENAS ♫ YO NO KIERO NADA ♫ LO UNICO KE KIERO ES KE AYA EN MI BELORIO UNA CERENATA POR LA MADRUGADA ♫*

10.06.15. all the files corrupted. google drive disappeared/erased/ eradicated. still, student snapchatting a new hole in separation barrier. I must plan for deviated futures. learn to play tuba? buy a drone?

11.06.15. rained today but I had my bonnet on. my belt buckle with the little pistol rusting. formulas of hospitality, in this country. man at café wants to learn spanich. "al chile" —"prender el bote" —"no mames." ordered 6 shots of espresso in drip coffee with heavy cream (they call it "the bracero lindo"... NFWA and chávez motif all around but also random ché quotes framed: *Déjeme decirle, a riesgo de parecer ridículo, que el revolucionario verdadero está guiado por grandes sentimientos de amor* and the favorite, *Hay que endurecerse sin perder jamás la ternura* for instance and one random photo of carnival in what looks like san cristóbal de las casas so what to do but close my eyes then and whispered *sonia.*

12.06.15. what's french sensibility? was gauguin virile inasmuch as machine with colonial fantasy? // I eat not a lot at all. days of love. arabic at 9 tonight. "I" have yet to "see" a "muslim."

13.06.15. saw avenida brasil on telemundo. KINDA GOOD. jorginho sleeping with maid while déborah doing some type of yoga on strings in air then falls and neck's hurt) all while shining my foot. my students come forth writing me: "who owns walter benjamin," "next year's green almond season," "othello." they like that he was black. they write, *we like the idea of a black king.*

14.06.15. opaque folklore.

15.06.15. begin building box but check if losing weight and height as was and been since before. also consider will I from sonia move or get going to? nonetheless keep factsheets of each test. need to sell motorcycle scraps. more mosquito repellents. more history books. more energy. more pleasure in general. more yogurts as well.

16.06.15.   sonia!
tehura! seafood! writing!
apartheid!   assholes!
grenades!   depressants!
pantheists! gym cramps!

17.06.15. problem is I get in the box who closes it. my stomach churns. been painting banana landscapes recently because they sell. master is silence. maybe if nail from inside with pointed leg?

18.06.15. weird that I dreaming again of disciple attention. like, firm stench. like, bent metal. like, those little sticks with the cottons on them. as if all setting forth and in exile again. either way my own tape around my wrists feel good. but the cop didn't do my gallows humor. what's the box for? sir, I go away there.

19.06.15. nothing to do but work.

20.06.15. petty idealist systems vs. foolish idealist complexes. the materials are scared and sacred. tonight have to rescind the classified ads even if pell-mell (Ω). wire transfer some money. I drink instant nescafé. guaraná run out.

21.06.15. where is gauguin book? did lose or did disappear? today in mailbox: *are militant atheists using chemtrails to poison the angels in heaven?* master texting with the word "peristalsis." cutting out the coupons carefully. sonia is not in jail. she is on chaturbate collecting tokens.

22.06.15. tonight set free the livestock. I'm living in the caloric way. filthy compositions. rarified acephalic and accelerated treasons. the unabridged contract; my declaration of independence. WHERE IS GAUGUIN BOOK?

23.06.15. found the gauguin! hidden under sleep mat. maybe I did? // on page 63: *Save me! Save me! / It is evening, it is evening of the Gods! / Watch close over me, Oh my God! / Watch over me, Oh my Lord! / Preserve me from enchantments and evil counsels. / Preserve me from sudden death, / And from those who send evil and curses; / Guard me from my quarrels over the division of the lands, / That peace may reign about us! / Oh my God, protect me from raging warriors! / Protect me from him who in erring threatens me, / Who takes pleasure in making me tremble, / Against him whose hairs are always bristling! / To the end that I and my soul may live, / Oh my God!*

24.06.15. box is not done. I saw false bait in the angel's banter: *pointy foot makes you thug hood.* forced into and now seemly. I doing rounds on rocinante. I lassoing with naproxen. on some days even starching for pressed crisp jeans.

25.06.15. saw american sniper. watched more avenida brasil. (ver-novelas-online.com) batata was born in landfill then renamed jorgito by carminha and tufão. remember donate to salvation army tomorrow. peeled the photos from the wall.

26.02.15. waiting for supplies. happening onto imported products. labneh, maftoul, red palm oil, emu palm wine, plantain fufu, cassava flower, bagoong, foco aloe juice, seaweed, orchids inarizushi no moto, shirakiku snow crab meat in water and now hungry. outside the store someone calls the fire department for an angry wasp nest. perfect time to steal and stuff in pants while vem dançar kuduro anthem in the shop. turns out lucenzo is french too.

27.02.15. in the archived. code section: 26 USC 5861 (d) case no. m-15-0877-m

28.02.15. swaddling the supplements. I like idea of wild fruit-ripe making musk. gauguin like all of them over time; parallelisms of fuckboy. "the autobiographical story." what can be compelling but also rightly answer? dover is SHIT. art is SHIT. spaceships are SHIT.

29.06.15. now if without nails, use glue. but no glue, so solid mud. the blueprints will become trash too. might as well go to ancient china. new-century poor blood bleeding. *knock knock. ¿No hay nadie? pregunta la mujer del Paraguay. Respuesta: No hay cadaveres.*

30.06.15. angry and stubborn will exist. 167.64 cm x 76.2 cm x 45.72 cm. hey stick leg! push off the top! hey dead fish! and the foaming sea!

*

I was compelled to return to France. Imperative family affairs called me back.

Farewell, hospitable land, land of delights, home of liberty and beauty!

I am leaving, older by two years, but twenty years younger; more barbarian than when I arrived, and yet much wiser.

Yes, indeed, the savages have taught many things to the man of an old civilization; these ignorant men have taught him much in the art of living and happiness.

Above all, they have taught me to know myself better; they have told me the deepest truth.

Was this thy secret, thou mysterious world? Oh mysterious world of all light, thou hast made a light shine within me, and I have grown in admiration of thy antique beauty, which is the immemorial youth of nature. I have become better for having understood and having loved thy human soul—a flower which has ceased to bloom and whose fragrance no one henceforth will breathe.

As I left the quay, at the moment of going on board, I saw Tehura for the last time.

She had wept through many nights. Now she sat worn-out and sad, but calm, on a stone with her legs hanging down and her strong, little feet touching the soiled water.

The flower which she had put behind the ear in the morning had fallen wilted upon her knee.

Here and there were others like her, tired, silent, gloomy, watching without a thought the thick smoke of the ship which was bearing all of us—lovers of a day—far away, forever.

From the bridge of the ship as we were moving farther and farther away, it seemed to us that with the telescope we could still read on their lips these ancient Maori verses,

Ye gentle breezes of the south and east
That join in tender play above my head,
Hasten to the neighboring isle.
There will find in the shadow of his favorite tree,
Him who has abandoned me.
Tell him that you have seen me weep.

What is your motto?

CRUDO SOY, BORACHO DE ESTE
SISTEMA

*What is for you the summit of
misery?*

JERUSALÉN

Where do you want to live?

HOTEL JUNGLA CARIBE

What is earthly happiness?

"EL SEXO DE UN ÁNGEL"

*For which faults do you fall into
formula?*

EL OCIO, TOMAR MI CAFECITO,
LEER EL PERIÓDICO

What is your favorite saying?

"AL NOPAL SÓLO SE LE ARRIMAN
CUANDO TIENE TUNAS"

What is your favorite acronym?

INRI: INSTIGADOR NATURAL DE
LA REBELIÓN DE LOS INFELICES

*Who are your favorite living
women?*

LA CHICA QUE SE LLAMA SONIA,

SELENA, JOYCE MANSOUR,
LEILA KHALED, MONICA MORÁN,
XEL-HA LÓPEZ MÉNDEZ, MIRENE
ARSANIOS, DEVANEE GONZÁLEZ,
MYA GUARNIERI, COMANDANTE
RAMONA, CAITLIN DÍAZ, CHARITY
COLEMAN, AMANDA TAWIL,
JENNIFER LÓPEZ CUANDO
INTEPRETÓ A SELENA, JENAN
KHALIL, HANNAH BAXTER,
MEGAN ESPOSITO, ORAIB
TOUKAN, MARYAM MONALISA
GHARAVI, LUCÍA HINOJOSA,
SAMANTHA JACOBUS, MELISSA
SIEBERT, CECILIA LOPEZ, NICOLE
DELGADO, KATIE KAPTAIN, LUCÍA
CENTURION, GABY CEPEDA,
LAURE DE SELYS, NASHLA DÍAZ,
MIS HERMANAS, MI MAMÁ,
MIS ABUELAS, Y MARÍA DE LOS
ÁNGELES FÉLIX GÜREÑA

*Who are your favorite fictional
women?*

SONYA

What is your favorite body part?

EL SOMBRERO

*What occupation do you most
enjoy?*

X

What person would you like to be?

LA CHICA QUE SE LLAMA SONIA

What ruins your day?

LA PALABRA NACO, PENDEJADAS
DE TODO TIPO

*Which flower do you want to be
when you grow old?*

FLOR DE PLÁTANO

What is the greatest unhappiness?

SER   POZOLERO,   TENER   QUE
CRUZAR EL PUENTE DE REYNOSA,
O EL CONTROL DE QALANDYA

*Who are your favorite heroes in
history?*

SONIA PERO TAMBIÉN MALINCHE
Y EL CUADRO NEGRO DE
MALEVICH

Do you like to kill?

PREOCÚPESE DE POR QUÉ A
ELLOS LES GUSTA MATAR TANTO

*What historical character do you
enjoy imitating daily?*

ŞALĀḤ AD-DĪN YŪSUF IBN AYYŪB,
RICARDO FLORES MAGÓN,
CANTINFLAS, MESSI

What military act do you most admire?

What military act do you most admire?

What military act do you most admire?

Do you think it is right that Israeli company Elbit Systems built the U.S. border wall?

PARA CULPARLOS DOBLE, SÍ

Would you return to Palestine?

DEPENDE

Why are you visiting the United States?

$$$$$$$$$$$$$$$$$$$$$$$$$$$$
$$$$$$$$$$$$$$$$$$$$$$$$$$$$
 $$$$$$$$$$$$$$$ $$$$$$$$$$$
$$$$$$$$$$$$$$$$$$$$$$$$$$$$$
 $$$$$$$$$$$ $$$$$$$$$$$$$$$
 $$$$$$$$$$$$$$$$$$$$ $$$$$$
$$$$$$$$$$$$$$$$$$$$$$$$$$$$$
              $$$$$$$$$$$

Where will you be staying?

POR LA 83

Who will you be visiting?

MASTER

How long will you be staying?

POR UN TIEMPO

How much money are you bringing?

$8.29, 78₪, €4.23, 82,576ل.ل
y 45 VAROS

Do any of the following apply to you? (Answer Yes or No)

A) Do you have a communicable disease; physical or mental disorder; or are you a drug abuser or addict?

SÍ

B) Have you ever been arrested or convicted for an offense or crime involving moral turpitude or a violation related to a controlled substance; or have been arrested or convicted for two or more offenses for which the aggregate sentence to confinement was five years or more; or have been a controlled substance trafficker; or are you seeking entry to engage in criminal or immoral activities?

"MORAL TURPITUDE"

C) Have you ever been or are you now involved in espionage or sabotage; or in terrorist activities; or genocide; or between 1933 and 1945 were you involved, in any way, in persecutions associated with Nazi Germany or its allies?

D) Are you seeking to work in the U.S.; or have you ever been excluded and deported; or been previously removed from the United States or procured or attempted to procure a visa or entry into the U.S. by fraud or misrepresentation?

SÍ

E) Have you ever detained, retained or withheld custody of a child from a U.S. citizen granted custody of the child?

NO

F) Have you ever been denied a U.S. visa or entry into the U.S. or had a U.S. visa canceled?

SÍ

What is your favorite color?

PURO NEGRO

What is your favorite food?

VUELVE A LA VIDA

*What gift of nature would you like
to have?*

TODAS LAS FLORES DEL ÁRBOL
DEL PLÁTANO Y UNA PLACA
QUE DICE "AUNQUE ME
CONSIENTAS CON REGALOS Y
LUJOS TODO ESTO PERTENECE A
LOS MUERTOS"

*What god or goddess would you
like to meet?*

XOCHIQUETZAL

How would you like to die?

LUCHANDO CONTRA EL ESPACIO
GRINGO

*What is your present state of
mind?*

—

ACKNOWLEDGMENTS

Parts of *gauguin's notebook* borrow from, or are inspired by, Oswald de Andrade, Julión Álvarez y su Norteño Banda, Kazi Nazrul Islam, Chalino Sánchez, Paul Gauguin, Roque Dalton, Paul Blackburn, Los Crudos, Néstor Perlongher, the 2015 Index of Economic Freedom, the Global Incident Map, the U.S. Department of Homeland Security's Electronic System for Travel Authorization, Wikipedia, various bibles, WebMD, The Red Army/PFLP: Declaration of World War, and Harddawn.com.

Excerpts of *gauguin's notebook* appeared in *X Poetics* and *The Fanzine*. The forum appeared in its entirety as part of Hypertext, a group exhibition curated by Intelligentsia Gallery and The Door Art in Beijing on April 24th, 2016. The June entries were published as an untitled chapbook with images by Barbara Ess for a special collaboration on the occasion of The Limited Sphere, a group exhibition at 321 Gallery, curated by Peter Brock in Brooklyn on January 30th, 2016.

I wish to express my sincerest gratitude to Robert Archambeau, Anselm Berrigan, Peter Brock, Joshua Corey, Luisa Espinosa-Lara, Cruz García & Nathalie Frankowski, Robin Tremblay-McGaw, Joyelle McSweeney, Dominique Yuki Mendez, Thalia Morin, Madeleine P. Plonsker, Davis Schneiderman, Eleni Sikelianos, Ernesto Solis Jr., Hugo Sosa, Ed Steck, Roberto Tejada, Rachel Tenuta, my friends and family from the Rio Grande Valley, and also the faculty, staff, and students of al-Quds Bard Honors College. I would also like to thank my dear friend, Mirene Arsanios, who saw and commented on many nascent versions of *gauguin's notebook*.

AUTHOR

Christopher Rey Pérez is a poet
from the Rio Grande Valley of Texas.
He currently lives and works in the
Occupied West Bank of Palestine.